FORTH and CLYDE
The Comeback Canal

by
Guthrie Hutton

Although the canal is famous for its little pleasure steamers, cleaned up barges were also used for Sunday School trips and works outings. This one may date from the late nineteenth century before the pleasure steamers became established.

© Guthrie Hutton 1998
First published in the United Kingdom, 1998
by Stenlake Publishing
Telephone/Fax 01290 551122

ISBN 1 84033 034 1

A party of First World War soldiers pass Cadder on the pleasure steamer *Gipsy Queen*.

The Comeback Canal

The Forth and Clyde Canal was a compromise between a ship canal to enhance the prestige and commerce of Scotland, and a barge canal to bolster the trade and wealth of Glasgow.

Work on the canal began at the eastern end in June 1768 with John Smeaton as engineer. After five years the cutting reached Kirkintilloch and trading began, with goods to or from Glasgow making the rest of the journey by cart. Two years later the canal had reached Stockingfield near Maryhill, but by that time the Canal Company had run out of money and work ground to a halt. Seizing their opportunity, Glasgow's merchants paid to have the branch canal cut into Hamilton Hill. It was completed by 1777 and gave the city's men of commerce all that they had ever wanted; a canal to the east coast to complement their river to the west. Glasgow prospered while the rest of Scotland's commercial interests fretted in frustration. They tried to persuade the Government to help, but it took eight years before funds from forfeited Jacobite estates were granted to complete the canal from Stockingfield to the Clyde.

Work began again in 1785 under a new engineer, Robert Whitworth. It was finished five years later. At the same time the Glasgow Branch was extended to a new inland harbour called Port Dundas.

The canal transformed communications and thrived as industry and commerce were attracted to its banks. It survived railway competition and ownership in the nineteenth century, but when the Admiralty closed the Forth Ports during the First World War much of its trade was destroyed and decline set in. It struggled into the 1960s, when its narrow, opening bridges were seen as an impediment to the new transport god, the motor car. It was closed on 1st January 1963.

For the next three decades it languished as a derelict, decaying, partially culverted mess, while voluntary groups campaigned for its restoration. In the 1980s the local authorities adopted a Local Plan that recognised the canal's value and started a process of improvements to bridges, lock gates and the towpath. In 1997 a grant of money from the National Lottery, to complete its restoration, was approved by the Millennium Commission and a year later the final pieces of a complex funding jig-saw were put in place. The canal had come back from the dead.

Guthrie Hutton, 1998

The puffer, *Porpoise*, heads east through Lock 37, Old Kilpatrick.

Canal Locks, Old Kilpatrick.

In 1790, twenty-two years after cutting began, the canal was opened to its western terminal at Bowling. The first vessel to travel from coast to coast was a naval sloop called the *Agnes* which sailed from Leith to Greenock through the canal. In later years, puffers, those little boats made famous in the stories of Para Handy and the *Vital Spark*, were a common sight at Bowling. Here the *Texan* heads from the inner to the outer basin through the delicate-looking timber bascule bridge and the massive stone abutments of the Caledonian Railway swing bridge in the foreground. The railway brought coal to Bowling for the puffers to ship onwards to coastal destinations, and while coal went out through Bowling, timber came in.

Much of the imported timber was simply lashed together like a raft and towed to canalside sawmills. The towing horses were stabled a mile to the east of Bowling, in the low building to the right of this cottage at Ferrydyke. The Roman fort, built to guard the western end of the Antonine Wall, was close to Ferrydyke Bridge, which appears to have been placed on the line of the Roman road that ran behind the wall. The road continued down to the Clyde and it is possible that the Romans could have operated a ferry from here to their large fort at Bishopton on the other side of the river. If true, this combination of Roman wall and ferry could be the origin of the name. In later years Ferrydyke was one of many points from which ferries crossed the Clyde before the main crossing between Old Kilpatrick and Erskine was established.

BARCLAY CHURCH OLD KILPATRICK

Old Kilpatrick's claim to be the birthplace of Patrick, Patron Saint of Ireland, is not universally accepted, although none can deny its strong religious associations. Kilpatrick was a single parish until 1649 when it was split into West and East, or Old and New parishes. The Old Kilpatrick parish church, which dominates the village and dates from 1812, is thought to be the third on the site. Despite this long tradition, 'the Disruption', the schism that split the Church of Scotland in 1843, deprived Old Kilpatrick of its minister when Matthew Barclay seceded to the new Free Church with some of his congregation. They established the Barclay Free Church, seen here behind the canal bridge. The bridge, which gave access to the Erskine Ferry slip, was replaced by a steel swing bridge in 1934.

Before the advent of steam, the principal means of moving boats on the canal was to tow them with a horse, although in a favourable wind some boats negotiated the canal's twists and turns under sail. The practice continued, even after steam had become established, as this picture of a fishing boat to the west of Dalmuir West bridge shows. The feat of navigation is perhaps even more remarkable given that the boat's Dublin registry might suggest a crew unfamiliar with the canal. Fishing boats from the east coast of Scotland often used the canal to move to the west, but a boat from Ireland going east is unusual, unless she was just coming into the canal to sell fish at one of the canalside towns. A boat returning to Fife made the last sea to sea passage of the canal on Boxing Day 1962.

Dalmuir from the Canal

The distinctive wooden bridges that spanned the canal were known as bascule bridges, from a French word which means see-saw. It aptly describes of the way they operated. The heavy bridge decks, counterbalanced by underground weights, were raised and lowered by a bridge keeper on one side and one of the passing boat's crew on the other. Each turned the impressively large cast iron cog mechanism with long lever handles. Although superficially similar to the others, the bridges at major roads were broader and heavier, like this one at Dalmuir which took the main Dumbarton to Glasgow turnpike road over the canal. It is seen here with the lighter *Westernlight* working through with a load of timber battens.

The slightly arched wooden canal bridges formed barriers to the development of electric tramway systems. At Dalmuir, trams from Dumbarton terminated on the west side of the bridge while Glasgow trams stopped to the east. The situation was resolved in 1915 when, after years of arguing over who should pay, the Dalmuir Bridge was replaced by a swing bridge. (Kilbowie Road Bridge was replaced at the same time too.) It allowed Glasgow trams to carry on to Dalmuir West, but in the car mad 1960s, trams and canals were both found guilty of impeding free movement of motor vehicles. They suffered an almost simultaneous demise. Glasgow's last tram, the No. 9 Auchenshuggle to Dalmuir West, was withdrawn in September 1962 and three months later the canal was closed.

When the canal was working, Clydebank folk could buy fish straight from boats like the Leith registered *Harvester* beside Kilbowie Road. It was cheaper and fresher than today's plastic wrapped supermarket alternative! Singer's sewing machine works, in the background, contributed to the canal's most enduring fishy story by letting warmed cooling water into the canal. It created ideal conditions for a colony of goldfish that thrived in the canal for years and provided boys with a steady income from selling them to pet shops. Clydebank's fishy traditions are continued by Scotland's first (and only?) floating fish and chip restaurant beside the Argyll Road Bridge. (It actually sits on the bottom of the shallowed canal, but as any good journalist will tell you, the truth only spoils a good story!)

In the early twentieth century, when this picture postcard was produced, the little country village of Drumchapel was the sort of place people went to for a holiday. One of the main attractions would appear to have been the four Boghouse locks, half a mile to the south of the station. It must have been a pleasant stroll down the Yoker road to Lock 35 where, with a bit of luck, a boat could be seen working its way up or down the flight. The road was carried over the canal on a bascule bridge which the canny canal builders placed across the lock chamber. It saved the cost of building separate bridge abutments and was done at a number of the locks. Housing now fills the open countryside behind the lock here.

The bridge taking Great Western Road across the canal at Cloberhill was replaced in 1930 by a huge lifting bridge. It was built by Sir William Arrol and Co. Ltd. as part of a major road improvement scheme and is seen here in the early stages of construction with concrete piles being driven in to support the new towpath. The timber walkway acted as a towpath while work was going on, but a guy rope, stretched across the canal to support the pile driver, apparently caused problems for boats' masts. The bridge was the first of its kind in Scotland, seventy feet wide and counterbalanced by weights totalling three hundred tons. The deck was ten feet above water level which let barges pass under without disrupting road traffic, although it had to be raised for the passage of masted vessels.

The original bascule bridge at the top of Crow Road, Temple, went across the chamber of Lock 27. As motor traffic increased in the 1920s, it became such a serious bottleneck that a policeman had to control the movement of vehicles, pedestrians and farm animals across it. After years of debate, work on a new lifting bridge, similar to the one at Cloberhill, began in 1930. It was part of a larger scheme to improve the road between Anniesland and Canniesburn Toll. The new road was opened in 1932 cutting a swathe through Robinson Dunn's timber yard, one of many such yards in the Glasgow area. With timber coming in through Grangemouth and Bowling the canal was the natural location for the trade and floating logs, like these narrowing the channel at Temple, were a common sight. The logs were kept in the water to maintain their moisture content as they seasoned.

Govan Cottage Bridge at the foot of Cleveden Road, Kelvindale, was named after a long forgotten dwelling. The cottage seen here was built later, at a time and in a style that reflects the canal's one time railway ownership. The bascule bridge carried some heavy traffic, but was never upgraded. In 1932 it broke under the weight of a steam waggon carrying clinker from the Corporation's refuse destructor. The waggon wedged itself on the damaged structure and because it did not fall in, both it and the bridge were removed for repair while the canal continued unaffected by their plight. *Polarlight*, the puffer heading west through the bridge here, was the second vessel owned by Ross and Marshall Ltd. to bear the name. She was built for the Admiralty in 1943 as fleet tender *VIC 26* (VIC is an acronym of Victualling Inshore Craft).

Mary Hill was an impecunious heiress whose fortunes changed when the canal was planned to come through her Gairbraid Estate. She feued ground for the growing canalside village on condition that it took her name. Before that it had been known as Kelvindock or simply the Dock, but Maryhill grew into a busy community with boatyard, timber yard and other typical canal-related industries. This picture probably dates from the late nineteenth century and appears to show the top two locks, Nos. 21 and 22. If so the buildings beside the top lock would be part of the Kelvindock Chemical Works, one of two chemical works alongside the locks. Behind the Kelvindock works was a spelter works. Spelter is a copper/zinc alloy used in 19th century metal fabrication, plumbing and for casting ornamental statuettes.

The eastern boundary of the infant Maryhill village was the aqueduct over Maryhill Road known locally as the 'Pen Bridge'. A hundred years later Maryhill had expanded almost to Queen's Cross and the original aqueduct, built in 1785, was proving too small for Glasgow's rapidly expanding tramway system. It was replaced by this much larger aqueduct in 1881. The new aqueduct was built beside the old one and the canal was re-cut through a sharper S-bend to go over it. The banks apparently burst while this work was going on and the local Police Chief took to the flooded Wyndford Street (as this part of Maryhill Road was known at the time) on an upturned kitchen table to direct the emergency. Gairbraid Church, just out of picture on the left, lost part of its grounds to the realigned canal.

Despite appearances *Clydegate* was no ordinary puffer: she, and an older boat called *Perfection*, were actually oil tankers. They were operated by the Anglo-American Oil Company (which later became Esso) from their Bowling terminal. The boats worked through the canal to the Forth and supplied fuel to garages on the west coast. Shell Oil also operated a tanker barge on the canal called *Mexdee*. Here *Clydegate* is passing the Ruchill Sawmill just to the west of Firhill Bridge. There were a number of sawmills in the Firhill area and the large kidney shaped basin to the east of the bridge was used as a timber pond. The bridge keeper, Jock Young or 'Jock the Briggie', was a 'weel kent' local character who was never done warning children of the dangers of playing on the floating logs.

Unlike their English counterparts, Scottish canal families did not live on their boats although men like these could spend days at a time working and sleeping on their plain, unadorned and often anonymous craft. The smaller barges were known as scows and could also navigate the Monkland and Union Canals. Lighters were bigger, and when not steam powered, required two horses to tow them. This Carron Company scow has had its hold built up with boards to take more coal than would otherwise be possible. It is sitting at the eastern end of South Speirs Wharf with the pleasure steamer *May Queen* behind. The steamers' berth, in front of Port Dundas House, was adjacent to the Ann Street Bridge. It sat at the top of the steep hill that generations of Glaswegians climbed on their way to join a canal cruise.

Drink played a large part in the boatmen's itinerant lifestyle. The canal had such a reputation for hard drinking that Britain's first temperance movement was established in Maryhill, and Kirkintilloch folk declared their town dry in a famous deed poll. The Canal Boatmen's Institute in Port Dundas Road was also set up to wean errant boatmen off the demon drink. It was staffed by volunteers from local churches and provided a heady mixture of religious services to feed the soul, and tea - with cakes left over from one of the local bakeries - to feed the mortal man. There were Saturday night tea meetings, Sunday services and on New Year's morning the volunteers turned up at six o'clock to serve a free breakfast to the boatmen's children. The boatmen were presumably on another planet at the time!

The way in which canal boats were built to fit snugly into locks and bridge holes is amply demonstrated in this picture of the pleasure steamer *Gipsy Queen* easing through Lambhill Bridge. The bascule bridge here was replaced by a lifting bridge in 1930. Behind the bridge, on the left, is the Lambhill Ironworks which started operations in 1881 and survived for just over a hundred years. It had a wharf on the canal which can also be seen behind the bridge. Lambhill was where town met country, although the 'countryside' to the east was punctuated with mining villages and pit-head frames. There was mining to the north of the bridge too where the Summerlee Iron Company worked ironstone at their Blackhill pits.

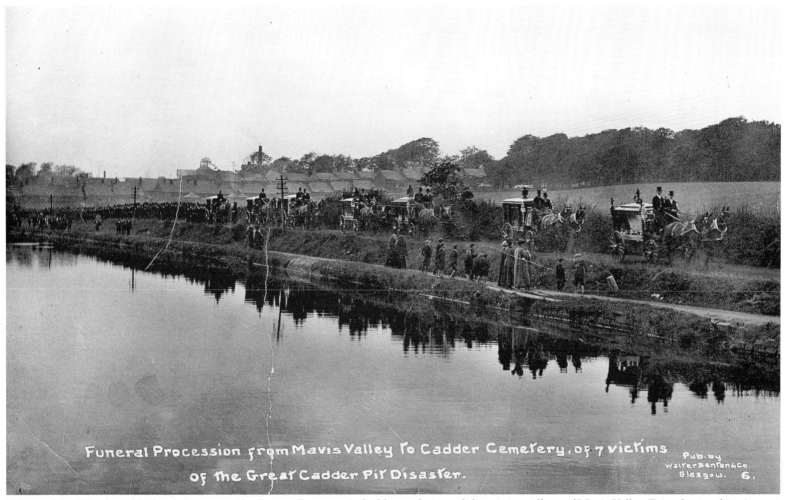

Funeral Procession from Mavis Valley to Cadder Cemetery, of 7 victims of the Great Cadder Pit Disaster.

Pub. by Walter Benton & Co Glasgow. 6.

Between Possil Loch and Bishopbriggs were the Carron Company's Cadder coal pits and the mining village of Mavis Valley. Tragedy struck in August 1913 when an underground fire in No. 15 pit trapped twenty-three men. Poisonous gas forced local miners to wait for trained rescuers from Cowdenbeath. They got one man out alive, but the other twenty-two had succumbed to the effects of carbon monoxide gas, known in mining as whitedamp. Most of the victims were from Lambhill and were buried there, but seven were from Mavis Valley. The village can be seen behind their funeral procession, here heading along the road beside the towpath to Cadder Church. The picture was taken just to the west of the present day Bishopbriggs Leisuredrome.

After sailing past industrial city suburbs and the mining communities beyond Lambhill, passengers on the pleasure steamers could look forward to the pretty village of Cadder. There was not much to it, but after the noise and grime it was idyllic. There were picturesque whitewashed cottages beside the canal bridge, the old mill and, set back behind leafy trees, the historic church. It was a favourite spot. A romantic one too, because here, screened from the outside world by rows of mature trees and with distant views of the Campsie Hills a young couple could dream, for a moment, that they were cruising on some exotic distant ocean - and all for two bob a head (tea was extra!). Here the steamer *Gipsy Queen* is seen having just passed Cadder on her return journey to Glasgow.

Taking an unwieldy scow, like this one, round the sharp bends east of Cadder Bridge could be difficult, as John Watson, the teenage son of a local mine owner, learned in 1836. He and a boatman left Kirkintilloch Hillhead basin at two o'clock one dark November morning with a laden coal scow. John was leading the horse, but before they got to Cadder the boat had gone aground twice and John realised that his companion was drunk. He could do nothing, except hope for the best, but just before the bridge the boat grounded again and started to sink. Working fast with ropes and pins they managed secure it to the bank, but the boy's father had to pay the Canal Company a high price to salvage the boat and cargo. Young John later founded his own coal business, becoming one of the foremost coalowners in Lanarkshire. He erected a memorial fountain in his native Kirkintilloch that still stands in the High Street.

The tall black and white funnel on this boat approaching Hungryside Bridge was typical of the steam lighters owned by the Leith, Hull and Hamburg Steam Packet Company. Their distinctive appearance was compounded by the company's policy of using a letter of the alphabet to identify them, instead of a name. Hungryside Bridge took the Torrance Road across the canal. It was closed briefly to road traffic in 1929 after being hit by a boat. Bus passengers from Glasgow had to alight at Glasgow Road Bridge outside Kirkintilloch and walk back to Torrance along the towpath. The incident hastened the end of the old wooden bridge which was replaced by a steel lifting bridge in the mid 1930s. It was built by Sir William Arrol and Co., and while it smoothed out the road, it created a dangerous blind double bend on the canal.

The Monkland and Kirkintilloch Railway was laid in 1826. It brought coal to a large basin on the western side of Kirkintilloch for onward shipping on the canal. In 1902 Peter McGregor started to build ships on a spit of land running into the centre of the basin. The yard had five building berths and produced a wide variety of vessels. Some, too big for the locks, were built in sections for reassembly outside the canal - giving rise to the suggestion that they were the longest boats in the world, with the bow in Bowling and the stern in Kirkintilloch! The picture shows two of eight pioneering motor coasters that were built at the yard in 1912/13. Their names all started with 'Innis' - *Innisbeg*, *Innisdhu* etc. The yard closed in 1921 and although no building records exist, up to 118 vessels are believed to have been built at it.

Boat operators J & J Hay repaired and maintained their own vessels at this slipway just outside the Monkland and Kirkintilloch transhipment basin. They also built boats in an operation that occupied most of the offside bank up to Townhead Bridge and provided constant work. When there were no boats to repair, there was always one on the stocks for the men to build. From the 1890s the Hay's named their puffers after warriors or tribes; *Gael, Tartar, Dane* etc.; the *Inca* and *Kaffir* were built in 1938 and 1944 respectively. By the late 1950s the company was feeling the pressure from road and rail competition and began scrapping some boats and converting others to diesel. The *Slav*, originally launched at Townhead in 1932, was the last puffer to be taken up the slip for repair. Her return to the water in November 1961 signalled the end of the boatyard.

Puffers have become part of Scottish folklore through the stories of Para Handy and the *Vital Spark*, and as J &J Hay probably contributed most to their development, Kirkintilloch can claim to be their home port. Equally, the town's puffermen can claim to be role models for the larger than life fictional characters. Here, watched by some children, a Para, Dougie, MacPhail or Sunny Jim leans on the aft railing of a puffer beside Hay's workshops and moulding loft. The boats were launched sideways into the canal from a building berth between the workshops and Townhead bridge. The last launch was in 1945 when the *Chindit* made a reluctant entry to the water. To launch the boat, two restraining ropes had to be cut by axes, but one axe shaft snapped and with only one rope cut the vessel slewed on the slip and stuck in the mud - an inauspicious end to a grand tradition!

When canals in colder countries ice over, skaters use them to move quickly from town to town. Such hard freeze-ups are rare in Scotland and these skate less Kirkintilloch folk appear to have ventured onto the canal at Townhead Bridge to let the photographer show how unusually ice bound it has become. Such an activity would be frowned on today because ice can be very dangerous and there have many tragedies caused by people venturing onto it - and not just on canals. On this occasion the freeze-up was either very hard - possibly the severe winter of 1895 - or occurred during a holiday, because there has been no obvious attempt to break up the ice for boat traffic. Townhead Bridge, in the background, was replaced by a steel swing bridge in June 1933.

The first of James Aitken's pleasure steamers was named *Fairy Queen*. She started service in 1893 and proved such a success that after only four seasons a new *Fairy Queen* took over. This picture shows *Fairy Queen I* heading west through Kirkintilloch's Hillhead basin. The section of canal from Grangemouth to the basin was completed and opened for traffic in 1773, making Kirkintilloch Scotland's first inland port. Boats arriving in the basin from the east had their cargoes transferred to carts which took them on to Glasgow, and in return delivered loads from Glasgow for the barges to ship back to the east. The Hillhead bascule bridge, seen behind *Fairy Queen I*, was replaced by a steel swing bridge in 1938.

When winter weather hampers today's road users, they accuse the authorities of incompetence and stupidity, until a scattering of grit and salt soothes their wrath and gets the traffic flowing again. It was never that easy on canals which could be brought to a standstill by ice. Sheet ice posed as big a danger to wooden hulled boats as the iceberg did to the *Titanic* and so the crews of fishing boats, which were not built for this fresh water hazard, had to protect the boat's hulls with iron sheets. Here two boats are heading east behind the protective bulk of the dredger *Clydeforth*, whichdoubled as an ice breaker in winter. The picture was taken from the Twechar colliery railway bridge which was permitted to be built only after the colliery's owners agreed to send coal by canal to the Dawsholm gasworks at Maryhill.

TWECHAR·BRIDGE

Twechar Bridge was between the railway bridge and its parent colliery, which can be seen in the distance on the left hand edge of the picture. The bus stop beside the bridge became Twechar's main link with the outside world when Alexander's buses started to operate to it from Kilsyth. The railway could not compete: the station was on the Gavell Road and although latterly named Twechar was actually closer to Queenzieburn. The buses stayed on the canalside road and did not cross the bridge into the village; nevertheless they provided a much needed link with the outside world for the relatively isolated villagers. Buses finally ventured across the canal when the old bridge was replaced by a new lifting bridge. It was opened in October 1960, two years and two months before the canal was closed.

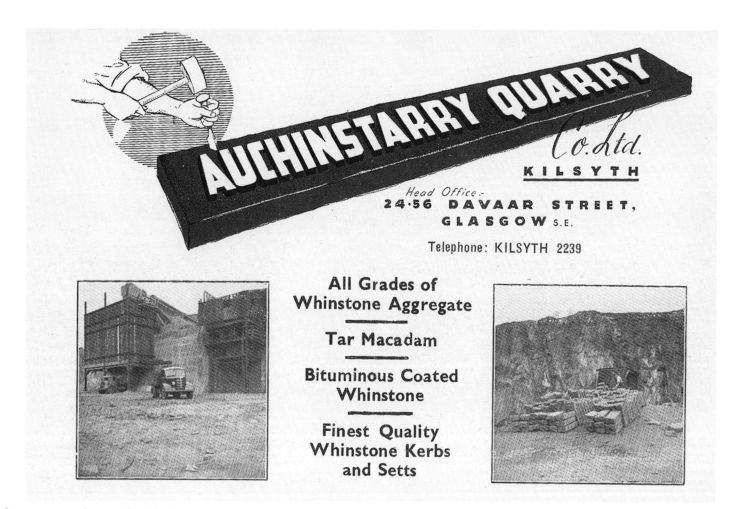

Auchinstarry was the port for Kilsyth and people clearly came a long way to join boats there, like the man from Ballinluig in Perthshire who named Kilsyth, Ontario, after this last bit of Scotland that he trod. The village of Auchinstarry, clustered around the bridge on the south side of the canal, was sustained by coal mining and quarrying. The quarry was impressive and was once a major canal user, sending its whinstone kerbs and gravel to Glasgow by the barge-load. It closed in the 1960s and has now been landscaped into a park where rock climbers hone their skills on the old quarry walls. Auchinstarry Bridge on the main Kilsyth to Airdrie Road was replaced a by steel swing bridge in 1938. The Forth and Clyde Canal Society based their trip boat, *Gipsy Princess*, in the nearby basin in 1990.

Fairy Queen II, seen here leaving Craigmarloch, was built at Paisley in 1897 by J. McArthur and Company. She replaced *Fairy Queen I* despite being much the same size and shape and having the same pale blue hull and red and black funnel. Outwardly the most obvious changes were a mast and a small deck cabin amidships; but the most important improvement for the helmsman was the wheel position in front of the funnel. This must have made steering on some of the tight canal bends much easier. To begin with there were no facilities at Craigmarloch for the passengers and if the prospect of walking or picnicking did not appeal - and it rained sometimes(!) - they just stayed with the boat. People could also buy produce from the enterprising occupants of the canal cottages on the left.

Fairy Queen II was joined by a new 'sister' in 1903. She was the *May Queen*, built at McGregor's boatyard in Kirkintilloch. She is reputed to have been 75 feet long which, if true, would have made her too big for the canal locks. This would have presented no operational problems, if as seems likely, her sailings were confined to the canal summit. She had a yellow funnel and white hull, an attractive colour scheme that was also adopted for *Fairy Queen II*. The two steamers operated alongside each other taking day-time mid-week cruises to Craigmarloch or Kirkintilloch and evening cruises to Cadder. On Saturdays *Fairy Queen II* sailed to Kirkintilloch in the morning and Craigmarloch in the afternoon while *May Queen* took a public or charter cruise to Craigmarloch. She had a piano on board so that charter parties could provide their own entertainment.

When the *Gipsy Queen* took to the water in 1905 she was the largest vessel ever to sail on the canal. She was built at the Paisley yard of Bow, McLachlan and Company along similar lines to present day Channel ferries so that despite being much bigger than her smaller predecessors, she drew only half the amount of water. As well as adding *Gipsy Queen* to the fleet in 1905 James Aitken built the tea room at Craigmarloch. It was known as the 'bungalow' despite having two floors. Teas were served inside and ice cream etc. was sold on the verandah. An eighteen hole putting green, and swings for the children, all added to the facilities and popularity of the little resort.

The *'Queens'* reached the height of their popularity in those halcyon Edwardian summers before the First World War, but in 1912 *Fairy Queen II* was sold. As the war dragged on, *May Queen* was also sold. After the war the *Gipsy* carried on alone until 1923 when a motor boat, *Fairy Queen III*, seen in the background next to *Gipsy Queen*, was introduced. She was a faster less exciting boat which failed to catch the public's imagination, and she was taken off after only eight years. Various ideas to bolster the enterprise were tried, like combining cruises with return rail travel, or simply promoting Craigmarloch as a destination for charabanc trips without taking to the water at all. *Gipsy Queen* was scrapped at the start of the Second World War and a little bit of Scotland's folklore died!

Before Craigmarloch was established as the terminal for the pleasure steamers their cruises were often extended to the eastern end of the canal summit at Lock 20 at Banknock. Also known as Wyndford Lock, it is seen here with the lock keeper's cottage alongside and the Bankier Distillery behind. The distillery is one of a number of distinctive canalside buildings that were demolished after the canal's closure, but thankfully the cottage and an old hostelry on the other side of the lock have been saved from the vandals (official and unofficial) and restored as attractive dwellings. While showing what can be achieved they also underline what has been lost elsewhere, like the row of cottages at Craigmarloch, demolished in 1976!

Bonnybridge is tucked in below the canal embankment while High Bonnybridge is, as the name suggests, above the level of the canal. This height difference created access problems over the years which were initially solved by an aqueduct, known locally as 'the Pend'. It was a dual purpose structure with a burn flowing on top of a paved road surface. The footpath (for humans) was raised above the level of the water-covered road so that only the horses' feet got wet. Later, as industry developed, the road was re-routed up the hill and over the wooden bascule bridge. The bridge was opened in 1900 and is seen here being crossed by the Bonnybridge Gala Day parade in 1908. It was replaced by a steel swing bridge in 1936.

Behind the parade on the previous page are Smith and Wellstood's Columbian Stove Works and Bonnybridge Foundry. The same buildings are seen behind the works' wharf in this picture, taken just to the east of the bridge. The scow appears to be loaded with crated castings ready for shipping on to customers. Iron was one of the canal's main industries with numerous works running up through Falkirk to Bonnybridge, Kirkintilloch and Glasgow. Lighters kept the works supplied with pig iron brought into the Grangemouth docks on ships from Tees-side. Lightermen supplying the Glasgow ironworks could work on a round the clock non-stop schedule that only allowed for sleep while the boat was moving on the longer pounds. It was a hard, unromantic life on the canal in those 'good old days'!

The best known lock on the canal is Lock 16 at Camelon, the top lock on the long climb up from Grangemouth. It is also the point where the old passenger boats terminated their run from Glasgow and where the Union Canal joined the Forth and Clyde. The junction basin between the two canals was known as Port Downie and the Union Inn was built beside it to cater for boat passengers. In more recent years the inn has become known as Auntie Kate's after one of its owners, Kate Struthers. It was run by the Struthers brothers, one of whom supported Rangers, the other Celtic and their division of the pub into rival halves amused many of the Falkirk supporting locals. The beer however was good and the pub filled customers' own bottles to take away, and boat crews' enamel pitchers to sustain them on their arduous onward journeys.

The *Arab*, the lighter emerging from Lock 15 in this picture, looks like an 'inside boat', a term used to describe a boat that only worked within the canal and docks. Such boats had no bulwarks, open holds and little freeboard, but they also had no masts, so the *Arab* might have doubled as a 'shorehead boat', one that also worked in the Clyde or Forth estuaries. Puffers that went 'deep sea' were known as 'outside boats'. Above the lock to the right was another canalside hostelry, the Canal Inn. In the late eighteenth and nineteenth centuries Camelon was a nail making centre, although the area around Lock 16 was better known for the usual canalside industries of iron and chemicals whose works can be seen belching out some heavy atmospheric pollution in the background.

234

The locks come thick and fast between Lock 16 and Bainsford. This one, with a horse-drawn scow being worked through it, is Lock 13. Working the locks was hard going and local boys could earn some extra pocket money by helping crews that had supped too long at the pubs around Lock 16. Yacht crews, unused to the ways of the canal, were also only too happy to pay for a little local expertise and muscle. Some boys were well organised bringing their bicycles with them for the journey back, but if they were really lucky they could pick up another boat at the other end and help to work it back. Fishing boats often arrived at Grangemouth with the whole family on board. The women and children helped to get the boat up to Lock 16 and then went home on the bus or train while the men carried on to the west coast fishing grounds.

The first of the canal's bascule bridges to be replaced by large steel swing bridges were at Camelon (above) and at Bainsford. They were built to allow Falkirk's new 'Circular' tram route to run from the town centre through Larbert and Stenhousemuir. The bridges caused a delay to the full opening of the route when the canal's owners, the Caledonian Railway, insisted on modifications to the cable gantries because they impeded the ropes of horse-drawn barges. The gantries were rebuilt with a cantilever across the towpath and the tram system was fully opened by March 1906. The modified gantry can be seen on the right, with one of Falkirk's French built trams crossing the bridge. Behind the bridge to the right is the Rosebank distillery's bonded warehouse - it is now a pub/restaurant; to the left is a typical canal warehouse.

Falkirk became famous through the nineteenth and early twentieth centuries as a centre for iron castings, and much of the industry, including the great Falkirk Iron Company, was concentrated beside the canal close to Bainsford Bridge. The foundries' product ranges included grills, gutters and drain-pipes, but more ornate products were made too, and although regarded as things of beauty today, the industry that created them was neither romantic nor pretty. Local people remember the canal near here as a smoke-filled canyon of dirt, noise and fumes. The bascule bridge was, like the one at Camelon, replaced in 1905 by a swing bridge for the new tram system. The pub on the right was known as the Red Lion before it was turned into an antique store; a conversion that would have had many an old canalman birlin' in his grave!

Locks 5, 4 and 3 gradually dropped the canal down from Bainsford to the flat land at Middlefield. The ground was easy and the navvies cut a wide and generous canal up through Grangemouth and the Dalgrain Bridge. Here, on the edge of Grangemouth's 'old town', an array of scows and lighters waits for work beside Canal Street. On the right, behind the fence, were the extensive timber basins. The town's position on the east coast and its canal link to the west made it Scotland's natural timber port. As in Glasgow the timber basins were a magnet for children. They loved to play on the floating logs which were lashed together and moved in unison, but children learned to look out for free floating or short ones that could tip them into the water. It was a dangerous game!

There was water everywhere in old town Grangemouth. To the west was the Carron River, to the north the docks, to the east and south the timber basins, and through it all ran the canal, like a main road - which of course it was when it was first made. 'Streets' like North Basin Street (above), and Canal Street (previous page), were more Venetian than Scottish, with front doors opening onto a quay rather than a road. The pub in the centre of the picture was named after the Earl of Zetland, the title of the descendants of Lord Dundas of Kerse, the first Governor of the Canal Company. It was one of many pubs and after closing time, men congregated around the basins and joined in impromptu fist fights, tug o' war competitions or sing songs. The bridge crossed the canal just below Lock 2. Beyond it, heading towards the Carron, was North Bridge Street.

Between them North and South Bridge Streets crossed three canal bridges, so they were well named. The bridge here is the one carrying South Bridge Street across the main entrance from the docks to the timber basins. With much of the canal's commercial traffic coming in through the docks, this lock and bridge were very busy, but compromises were needed to cram them into a restricted space. Instead of a ramp the steps on the left lead up to the lock sides where the lock gate balance beams are unusually short and stubby. The equally stubby lock keeper must have had to work hard to move them. The bascule bridges here, and across the other timber basin entrance, were replaced in 1938 although the bridge across the canal itself, in front of North Basin Street, was not replaced until 1951.

In its early years the canal attracted industry like a magnet, but as industry developed so did railways which soon threatened the canal. Competition between rail companies was intense, and in an attempt to draw trade away from the rival North British Railway, the great Caledonian Railway bought the Port of Grangemouth in 1867. It gave them a foothold on the east coast, but in buying the port they also had to buy the canal. It could have spelled disaster - canals taken over by railways were often killed off - but because most of the Forth and Clyde route was through North British territory the 'Caley' kept it going. Extensive Caledonian Railway activity can be seen in this picture of the Grangemouth docks taken from the most easterly of the entrances to the canal timber basins.